About the title:

I was told that my inner colour is silver, with the properties of absorbing, cleaning and re-polishing feelings. Now it is up to you to decide if I've succeeded.

First published in
2013 by Rashad Carre
Copyright © Rashad Carre

ISBN: 978-1-291-20803-0

The moral rights of the author have been asserted.

All rights reserved.

No part of this publication may be reproduced, stored in a retrieval system, or transmitted, in any form or by any means, without the prior permission in writing of the author, nor be otherwise circulated in any form of binding or cover other than that in which it is published and without a similar condition including this condition being imposed upon the subsequent purchaser.

Cover Illustration: Rashad Carre
Cover Design: Rashad Carre
Book Design: Rashad Carre
Illustrations: Rashad Carre

Produced through www.lulu.com

I dedicate this compilation of expressions to all those who believed in me, especially my mother, whose support and dedication has never wavered.

                                        God Bless you and thank you.

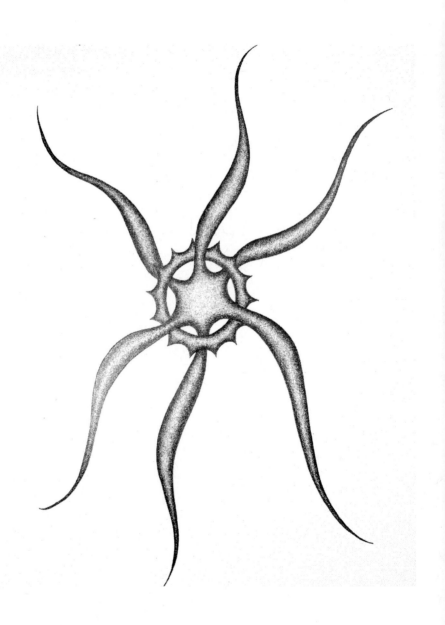

Verses

A quiet

Pensive

Ink drop

Of thought

Running courageously

Across the page

Linking line upon line

Of words

Bringing together

A multitude

Of symbols

Ideas

To be read

Thoughtfully

Pensively

Quietly

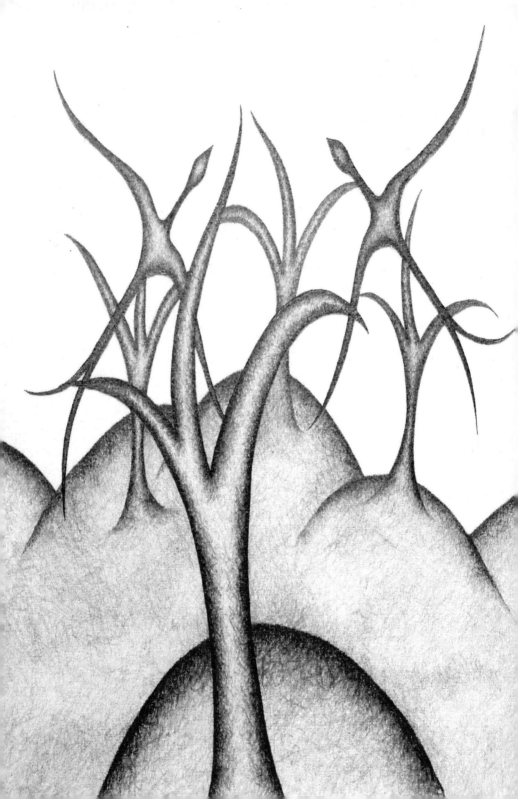

My Lover

Can I come with you, wherever you're going?
May I sleep with you in your bed?

I just want to hold you, caress you.
I want to talk with you late into the night.

Naked, side by side with nothing to hide,
Like when we were children, innocent.

I want to see your world, know your experiences.
I want to touch your lips as you tell me.

Each word you speak melts into my ears,
It tantalizes my imagination.

It gives me hope and laughter,
Your colourful lives of what was and what will be.

You lead me, like a guide through the desert,
Seeing each step reflected in the granules of sand.

You my inner heart, the window to my soul.
You are me, and I love you.

A Moment of Bliss

An afternoon at the beach.
The sun shines on the pebbles, heating my skin.
The waves crash on swimmers screaming with glee.

A breeze cools the heat.
Sunbathers come and go.
The water sparkles emerald green.

The blue sky sprinkled with clouds.
The feeling of being present so palpable, so delicious.
Sadness, loneliness, illusions of worry,
Stranded on the shores of concern.

Such utter beauty held in a moment of time.
Being alive to witness inner tranquillity;
This is true beauty, calm, unabated existence.

Patterns

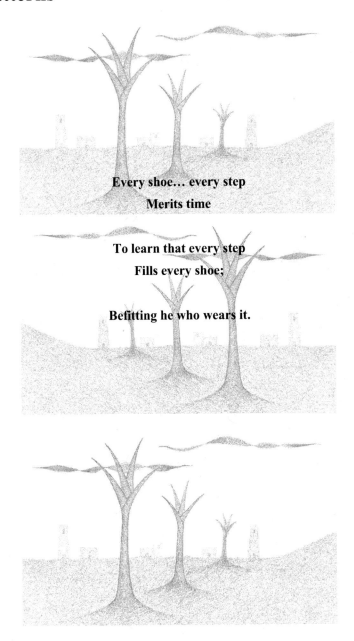

Every shoe... every step
Merits time

To learn that every step
Fills every shoe;

Befitting he who wears it.

The River

Mixed with sadness, I went looking for pain.
With cocktail in hand I toasted life.
Shaken but not stirred I tasted the bitter liquor.

I got drunk with the frenzy of what I was told.
Embellished words took on that haze of rose coloured truth.
Beautifully articulated, it tasted sweet on the palette of understanding.

I was swimming and diving through the waters of life.
Learning to hold my breath and how to come up for air.
A sport that was making me strong and fit for existence.

Even when I hit a rock, then 2, 5, 7, I kept up the fight.
After all I was alive with that bitter nectar of life,
Enhanced with the excitement of that never-ending juice.

Contd.

I even got used to that taste of sadness and pain.
I was rolling along and by God I was managing.
Ha, ha, look at me, I'm still alive!

The current pushed me to calmer waters and onto a sandbank.
I climbed out, and for the first time since I was very young, I was dry.
I breathed deeply and my head cleared.

A voice began to speak to me.
My voice, so strange, so foreign.
I started listening and I looked at my body, my mind, my heart...

I was scared at first
Scared to see what it is I had to say, to know what it is I would see.
But I felt calm, and I trusted that feeling.

I looked again at the river to which I did not want to return.
I knew I had to, it's where my destiny is, and I am bound to it.
But maybe, just maybe this time it can be different.

Fear

Acrid bitterness bites through my mind
And the pit of my stomach becomes an infinite gulley.

Walls of stone penetrate my veins,
Petrifying my soul.

But when sweetness slides across my tongue,
My heart is gently soothed.

The Unknown

In here everything is quiet
Friendly
Peaceful.

An unusual feeling that makes everyone silent.

For the reality of the world soon seeps in
Making them cautious
Harsh
Sad.

A Hug

Forgive me mother
I spoke with a crisp tongue.

The air is becoming cold again
Full of anticipation of the darkening light.

A time so alien to me,
One I never had to face as a child in your embrace.

Old Objects

Captivating objects of desire
Transform into little windows of the past
Opening a world of dreamy, watery memories.

Stories entrenched in poetic verses
Hidden in cupboards amongst the clothes,
Stacked on shelves you made.

I keep the precious trinkets,
The ones that remind me of holidays,
Exotic memories of laughter and confidence.

I want to forget the twisted frustrations of finding life,
But each new piece uncovered
Is like a demon burrowing in my heart.

Contd.

Just throw it all away!
Burn it, rip it up, start afresh.
Clear my heart and mind!

But some of the designs I drew, the poems I wrote, the photos I took...
No, those I keep.
You never know, there may be a genius hidden within them.

Is there not a masochist within each of us?
Just a little,
After all, people say it's pain which creates and joy that appreciates.

The love of Angels

The sun burst open yesterday.
It spat out its tormented dreams.
Man was twisted and tortured.
You slept through that day.
You had dreams full of angels.

Unknown Travels

The sun lavishly swallows up any moisture.
The animals made to melt into the shade.

The earth, dusty, barren and lifeless,
While cirrus clouds hush across to take a peak.

The languid light of dusk leads the day to the cool of night,
And a group of men slowly shake the dust.

Tempest

Man squashed the cricket
When he fell sway to his desires.

The cricket, now living, sings with delight
Freed of the pain we all know.

Let the flowers show where he lies,
Have the bees flourish of the pollen they offer.

So they may return ripe with food
That man may harvest their honey.

The Hunt

The lake floats high in the mountains
Silently reflecting the peaks.

The villagers gather along the shore
Waiting with hushed whispers.

Their eyes turn to the trees
As a fluttering of wings breaks the air.

An eagle takes flight,
Eyes dart back over the lake.

The surface begins to quiver.
Men, women and children hold their breaths.

A high pitched screech tears through the air
As the eagle begins to dive.

Fishing lines tumble into the lake
As the spawned fish jump in frenzy.

Howls of delight and sheer amazement burst forth
As the hunt begins.

The Air Of Dreams

The closed lattice door rustles
As the wind whistles through the cracks.

Ravenous for heat
Lifting all that is light and open.

It cools the passions,
Pierces the hidden dust of corners.

Like a hunter looking for the kill
It crawls up over the sheets.

Whispering into your sleeping ear,
It settles to play with your dreams.

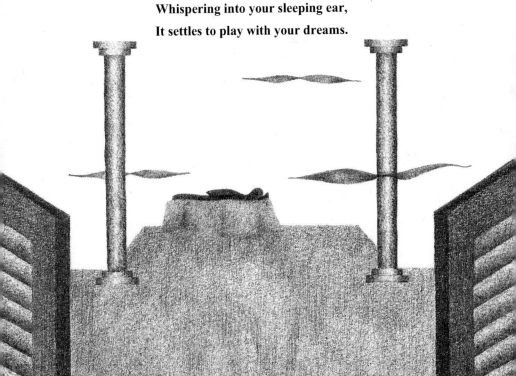

Age

The whispering regard
Of an old man
Who sits patiently
Waiting for the bus.

The cold air whistles past
Tussling his hair
Making it fall into his face
As his wrinkles scrunch up in a squint.

His elbows sag
Dragging down his body
His chin slouches on his hands
His hands rest on his walking stick.

Heavy with stupor, he rises.
He draws his hand
Through the few strands of hair
As the bus slides gently to a stop.

Life

A thunder in the distance
Whose echo makes you turn.

A beautiful scene invites you,
Cold and very lonely.

You walk in with all the beauty around you.
Sensational passion rips through you.

Woven into this beauty
You stand out as an intruder.

You want to leave desperately,
Yet you want to stay with all your heart.

Morning

The orange glow of morning takes your hand.
It whispers in your ear,
"It is time to rise."

The marbled floor, cool under your feet,
As warm water washes over your face
While your hand reaches for the towel.

You light a cigarette
While the percolator makes your coffee
And your eyes watch the fanfare of colour light the eastern sky.

But your day is made of sleep,
For your dreams are where you live;
Where you are sure of your love.

This Place of Oz

Your fingers stretch through the sky.
You see the earth reflected in its heart.

Your voice sings the words of your joy
As the ground undulates through its towering trees.

You watch the light cascade across the land.
You know this place, where the lake of your thirst is quenched,
Where your hunger is satisfied.

But you look to the ground and the sky
And you know the search for Love will take you on.

Mocking Disaster

Clouds of water fill the streets
As autumn's voice thunders through the wind.

Hands cup around their coffee
Harbouring in the shelter of a café.

Giggles of compassion welcome another drenched victim
As their clothing becomes revealing.

Voices twitter across the air
The room electric with consternation.

Whispers of "never before" rise from each table
Leading to a crescendo of the "end of the world".

The deluge ends as abruptly as it appeared,
Leaving the drains to accomplish their design.

The harbouring clientele smile,
Relieved and embarrassed as the atmosphere of doom dissolves.

And as I step out into the sun,
The mocking smile of a rainbow covers the sky of Paris.

More Than I Know

A full moon rises
Sensually awakening my sleep.

I grant the moon its favour
And surrender myself to its force.

My body begins to dance
Embracing the joy of an eternal friend.

I close my eyes.
I pray to meet him again.

I take the warmth of moonlight with me
To heat my bed and help me rest.

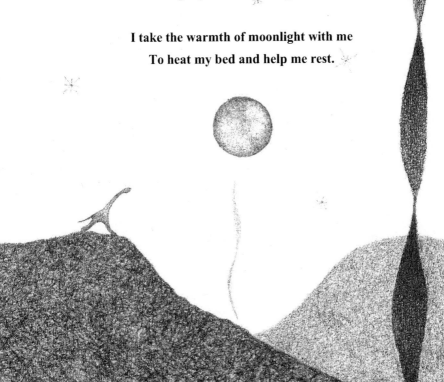

The Creative Man

You glide in the air of inspiration,
Your heart guides the impulse of your touch.

Like a cloud you wait for release,
The ground dry and impatient.

Succulent expressions ooze from your fingers,
Bringing to life many dreams.

People's emotions abound,
Fluttering like angels.

And you are but one amongst many;
Fools riding through the mass of hysteria.

Healing Love

Touch me gently with your furtive glances.
Let your fingers slide over me,
For you dance to the music of sensuality.

Your curves caress me as you move
And the rhythm penetrates
As you breathe new life.

Gentle thoughts invade me
Creative ideas flourish
My privacy is compromised.

Sweet, sweet and tender is this invasion.
You thrust a dagger in my heart of sadness.
Like a child reborn my eyes open with a smile.

Ego

Beauty stalks the streets
Tempting the imagination of hungry eyes.

The wind blows sensual waves of hair
As the sun reveals more and more of the body.

There the fire of passion is born
Pushing the loins of desire into a play of action.

The desire of human contact
The courage of vocal intervention.

An exchange ventured, a contact made.
Friendship found, albeit brief.

And so the human search continues
As it staggers in front of the mirror.

And dressed to impress,
It makes its way out the door.

Narcissism

Staring into the lake
My reflection clasps my eyes.

Burrowing my mind,
Rummaging through knowledge therein.

Crying out to indentify itself
In ever tightening circles.

Its deafening cry only heightened
By my pensive countenance sitting on the shore.

The water ripples
As my breath labours.

Peace comes as our lips meet
And waters of life unite us.

Worldly Tastes

Sensual delights tempt the palette.
Rosy cheeks set in a cluster of red curls.

The unending curves of the body
Enlaces in folds of silk.

Each erection set off by tender caresses of feather-light fingers
While the hush of lips breathe through the hairs of the skin.

The drip of an ice-cube trickles down the cleavage
As an arch of the back indicates delight.

A palette of rosy pleasure lightly flaked with gold
So tempting as to turn rose into red.

The blood of lusting desires overtaking reason
Driving fulfilment to obese abundance.

A testament imprinted in memories
Handed down through time.

A heritage of man's flesh
To become 'ashes to ashes' and 'dust to dust'.

Day Dreaming

A horn blasts from a bus
Belching black smoke
As the car in front moves on.

The smoke hangs in the air
Suffocating the sound of coughing
As she pushes through the crowd.

Aware of people's stares
Her almond eyes take a sideways glance
Quietly seductive.

She is shy and self-conscious
As the curves of her body
Glide with every step.

Contd.

Born with an eternal beauty
That cannot hide in drab clothing
Or unkempt hair.

Like Cinderella
Her fate is sealed
To marry a prince.

Her kindness will affect
The deeds of other men
To charitable means.

Her quietness
Imbuing peace to her surroundings,
Returning faith to the hearts of men.

Another blast of a horn
And the bus barely runs me over.
More smoke chokes everyone's throats.

The woman passes me
Muttering obscenities at the bus
While clearing her nostrils onto the side-walk.

The Mirror of a Memory

Sunlit wine trickles down my throat
As I gaze across the rolling hills.

A solitary figure breaches the crest
Standing with arms outstretched, ready to ride the winds.

He runs through the undulating paths of crumbling chalk
As a shadow glides over, willing to quench the earth's thirst.

A dove takes flight
As the hills shake with the clap of thunder.

The man quickens his pace,
His shadow seems to be the clouds rumbling with every step.

He opens the door just as the sky clears to let the sun come through.
He takes a glass and lets the sunlit wine trickle down his throat.

Recycling

A breeze flutters through my hair,
Cooling the scorching fire of the equatorial sun,
Making the pores of my skin shiver.

My eyes dart across the remnants of elegant trees
Seeing wild rose bushes in perpetual bloom
Pay homage to the wood many miles away.

Few birds fly or call to each other
Making sirens scream through the voices of cicadas
Following the lonely rustle of a grey squirrel.

My feet leave their mark in white granules of shimmering sand
As I turn to face the city, the digestion of this hunger,
To return the growth of many trees.

Winning and Losing

Is it so strange that love
Rests so lightly on the lips of men?

Wasn't it the common man
Who debased its meaning?

Love is life's truth
The rest are just tools of the trade.

The guise of truth is human relations
And the tool of this guise is work.

They are brothers, life and love,
That's why we hate and fear so much.

The rewards of love are bigger than life
So which do you think is going to win in the end?

A Little Kindness

An impoverished man seeks my hand,
I give him a coin for his hunger.

He asks for a little warmth,
I give him my coat.

He tells me he's thirsty,
So I buy a bottle and we share a drink.

His eyes begin to clear.
A smile creases his face.

I look into his eyes,
I know I have misunderstood.

The man is waiting for more,
My un-judged compassion.

All I could do is offer material concessions
For the love of God we call humanity.

Welcome

Fly with me to new frontiers
Where the flavour of roses glides with moonlight,
Where sight and sound is still.
Thought is open and miracles begin.
A miracle of feeling no fear.

A place grounded in truth
Where the sadness of narrow lives is chiselled away,
Where wealth and poverty walk hand in hand,
Where we are glass vessels as clear as crystal.
A place where journeys begin.

A whisper resounding in the vast emptiness,
Emptiness filled with light;
Light exuding life,
Life giving love,
Love opening great pathways so simple.

To be in heaven while we count money,
To be in heaven when we speak,
To be in heaven when we think,
To be in heaven in heartache.
To breathe in heaven with every breath.

The Graveyard of a War

The ground was once great
The people proud.
Now they are crushed,
The two in one.

They lie together
Their limbs intertwined.
No longer separate,
No longer dominant over the other.

Now they work together,
Not only to survive their souls,
But to stop the marching troops
Who are a part of life.

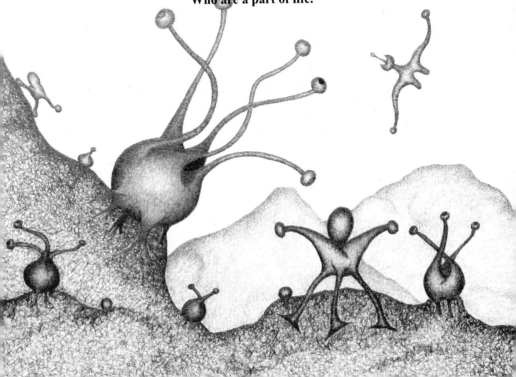

Meeting Life

The talk of mountains
Sounds through my chest
And I heave with excitement.

The heavy clouds clear,
Blown by the roaring wind
Giving way to the majesty of whispering stars.

They tell of a path
That winds through treacherous rocks,
Falling cliffs that tumble into the abyss of valleys.

Valleys carved through time
By delicate fingers of erosion;
Fingers that scratch at the surface of all things.

Contd.

My feet walk me forward
Listening carefully to the whispers,
Leading me to a wide future of hope.

The black sky of night
Puts to sleep the fears of wayward thoughts
Allowing dreams to flutter with happiness.

The mountain range begins
And daylight brings it to the sea
Where the waves greet it with thunderous applause.

The light cascades down through the heavens
Shadowing any doubt.
I kneel down to have known life.

Loss of Love

How long can I tread water
In this barren ocean that has replaced my heart?

The boat builders left;
Their creations resting below the surface.

The dredgers came and went
And the wind is still.

There is no current to carry me to shore
And the black sky is starless.

The only things moving are my arms and legs,
The only sound is my laboured breathing.

Will these cease,
Or will there be a new beginning?

Hope vanished
When the last seagull plunged to its death.

I'm thirsty and my body's getting cold,
But the waters will not claim me.

How long can I tread water,
And why?

Journey For Love

Lift yourself into the wind
Take flight.

Over cradled valleys
Past their smoking guardians;

There in the far reaches where we cannot go
Your madness awaits you.

Oh for the love of your voyage
The steam of your passing.

Only you of the Lord
Strong and capable.

There you will discover Love
Love from God, so inherent, so forgotten.

Exodus

The exodus of dying peoples
Turn their backs on a forlorn past.

Depressed eyes seek pleadingly through the crowds
Mixing with the dust of each footstep.

A child hangs on her mother's back,
Its lips chapped and limbs limp.

Rivers of wine and honey
Beckon their limbs to move forward.

Legends of peace and harmony
Loom larger than truth in their minds.

Contd.

The first leg of the journey
Unites them around the evening fire.

Freshly dug graves,
Milestones to the moving crowds.

Morning light lifts their hearts
As tombstones bless their resting place.

The remains of the tribes walk on,
Abandoned by death.

Hands of peace touch their faces,
Leading them to a dome of light.

Three days and three nights
Prayers sound within.

Men and women watch
As love blossoms across their lips.

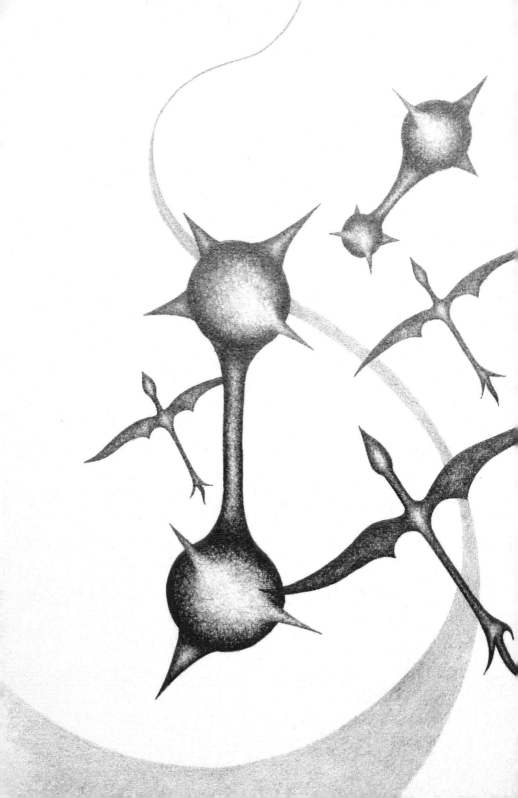

When The Changes Will Come

When the flame grows brighter,
    lit by the true love of a prayer.

When the coming of life into mankind
    is like a long lost legend brought to bear.

When water is driven by a fresh source
    coming to reawaken lands long left idle.

When the wind rises to the challenge,
    giving voice to its tempestuous nature.

When time creates new horizons,
    turning over a new leaf for the chapters of history.

When the earth abounds in the frenzy of anticipating change.

When it quivers to shed its old skin, tilling that which is stale.

Then it will be a time of change harbouring many blessings

When all we can do is witness it, opening our light to follow the change.

Where Am I

This small crack in my mind,
It looks at me longingly.

I poke my finger into it, just to see.
My finger moves around, expanding it.

I peak into it and see nothing.
I step back, contemplate.

The crack vibrates.
I look again, curious, more attentive.

I see a wet light far in the distance.
I hold my breath and plunge in.

It feels strange, not wet but liquid.
My eyes slowly adjust.

Contd.

Hazy images flow around me, intriguing me.
I reach out to find nothing there.

The light, again the light.
This time crisp, piercing and bright.

It calls me, I hear my name.
I move slowly towards it.

The hazy forms begin to clear.
These forms are me! Millions of me!

I feel them the more I move.
I begin to know them one by one.

I race towards the light, running, swimming, flying…
I start to laugh holding hands with my selves.

This is not my mind.
I'm in my soul, alive and aware.

The Mind

Run… run and hide in your contemplative mind.
Thoughts give you glory and riches,
Sipping on the dreamy liquid of inspiration.

For your way is the only way to the right way,
And no challenge is too great,
Not even that of God.

But, nobility lies in deeds,
And the one challenge impossible,
Is that of reality.

So choose wisely your little hole,
Where you crawl into at night,
Where you go to in times of need,

And where you seek to drink of the liquid of life.

Truth

A sage once said
"Life is not the bastard of Love
It is the honoured prodigy."

Our task is thus:
To take the prodigal son to its father,
Love.

Death

The final giving of all we have.
The enveloping return.
A return to our harmonious inner.
An inner that holds the essence of our past.

A cycle of all we are made of.
The doorway of calm to the hereafter.
A hereafter that holds no complications.
A pathway filled with the love of God.

Returning to where we came from.
To where our soul lives
To where we continue.
The awakening of our dream.

So Little We Know

Let there be life when death comes.
The life of angels and beyond,
There where we come to unite.
Where life begins.

Take care to follow its path,
The change will not wait for those who hesitate.
So flourish the ground within,
Recognition will come to those who know.

Suicide

The blinds are drawn
The day is ended
The covers turned for sleep.

Silence reigns through the air
Slipping in through the darkness
Sliding across your eyelids.

Peace is the order of this hour
Broken only by the questions in your mind
Repeatedly asking, "Why?"

The bottle lies empty
The pills spilled across the floor.
Soon you will be at rest.

So hush your fears
Your worries will be no more
For it was always only a matter of time.

Intangible Fears

Mistletoe grows wild,
Snow twinkles cold.

Clouds blow in heaven,
Roots planted in hell.

Smoke curls beautifully
Ashes to dust.

My eyes fill with tears...
So many thoughts misunderstood.

The Tears Have Not Come

A scream of anguish resounds in my chest
As my mind is pierced by the lance of its madness.

I lunge to defend myself from harm,
But my instincts strain.

The whirl of terror takes shape.
It sucks, pulls and lures me in.

The order of self-destruction is formed,
Rational, down to every detail.

But the waters have not broken,
And the birth of these tears may not come to pass.

Imagination's Sorrow

Thin beams of light break through the cold
Stretching across a barren plain.
Like empty hands cutting through rock
To plough the seeds of hope
And reap the love that trickles from dreams.

Dreams forgotten and created by time
To relieve the knots in our thoughts
And melt the stress into a new day,
The stress of time created for the fulfilment of our dreams
Generated by the hope of Love.

But our hearts break.
Our attention turns to the lonely one,
For we are saved by humanity
That returns again and again
To whisper gently through our souls.

Depression's Saviour

Pain is the beginning of this poem.
Pain that memory has banished.
Words lost in a deep chasm of the spirit.

A pain that haunts you like blood in your veins.
Like a raindrop in the ocean,
A raindrop that may have been a teardrop of generations past.

Such a decisive neglect,
One that started the ever growing world of ghosts,
Shadows lost in self-imposed hell.

Screams of anguish twisted tight.
Fear... it drowns, suffocates and crushes words.
Lungs gasp in this pain.

Contd.

There is no dictionary, no map, no philosopher's stone.
The pain, unique to each and everyone,
The true untold story.

It is only the soul, the essence of belief.
It has strength enough to go to the dark silence,
That silence which needs only listening.

A candle whose wax is love,
Divine love, with no retribution.
A light that shines eternally.

A light that links inexorably with the pain.
A light that will die without the healing of pain.
This is how the soul listens to that silence.

It brings fearless words to pain;
A consciousness to healing,
It bestows a will to be alive and loved.

A Plea

It hurts, your pain, your sadness ripping through me.
The sadness buried deep in your laughter.
My tears, they speak for you.

Your dreams have become nightmares from which you cannot wake.
Dreams full of hate and fear, lust and greed.
Dreams dressed up so magnificently, even you are fooled.

You seek shelter from the cold, but your voice is ice.
You seek the truth, but hide it deep in your heart.
You walk proudly, blind in your thick fog of confusion.

Have you not learned that the shepherd is you;
Why are you afraid of that shepherd?
It's your voice that can change things, but you keep it quiet.
It is your love that is drowning while you believe you are alive.

I stand like a sponge, drenched in your pain.
Your suffering is cruel for the pain you inflict in others.
We are all one in this human life walking this earth.

Please help dry my tears with your courage.
The courage to find that window to your inner heart.
It means you no harm, it is immaculate love.

Past Love

The narrow staircase showed you
The side entrance to my heart.

Do you ever cry
At the spot-lit love engraved in stone?

We put it there together
With a hammer and chisel.

That was a long time ago
When our hands embraced.

The wrong thing at the right time;
Selfish for our happiness.

I wonder about your heart
As I climb those stairs.

Do you pine for the train that takes me home
As I do for leaving the one that takes you?

We pretended happiness and love
And our pretence convinced us for awhile.

How fortunate that truth stood firm
For deceit and hate live hand in hand.

The End of a Time Together

Clench my hand with a tenderness that will not falter.
Our time together is brief and we have much to learn.
This love was only meant to open doors, not keep us together.

The tears shed will be so vast as to create a chasm of torturous pain.
The rage so loud as to echo for generations.
The madness of unknowing so blinding.

This will be, but never let it kill the love that holds me tender.
Wrap all that we were together in your protection.
Let those doors of discovery open wider to more that is waiting.

The twinkling lights of memory will guide us with our smiles.
As each of us journeys on to things so much wider than pain.
As we take one step for tears, one for laughter, we go on to new lives.

Verses of the Past

The verses have long past
And shall always return.

They peak out through open cracks
When people are careless.

Their impact little strong, but reliable.
Seeing their chance, and taking control.

But for all the pain they may bring,
They are not the demons of sadness.

They are reliable to the old,
Always comforting for their stories of childhood.

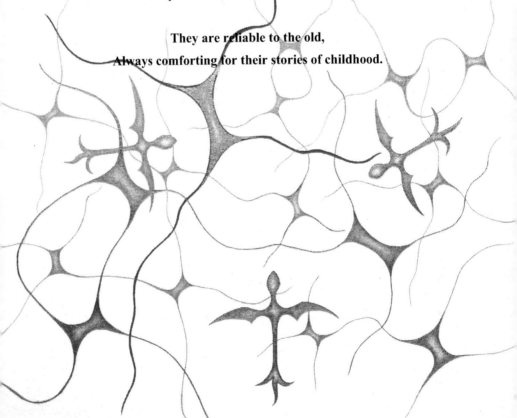

Precious Moments

Why is it we live but to love.
To find those moments when what we have inside can be real.
When it can reach out and say, "I exist."

To feel safe in being vulnerable.
A moment of respite from the mind and what it wishes for.
That mind and wishing constantly cautious.
Cautious from many a time when a word, a deed or a look throws
a dagger into the heart.

Those moments of love illuminate the existence of peace.
Moments unabashed by its own beauty,
Unashamed by its honesty and truth.

It is the truth of being alive and what we can give to life.
A way to give thanks and acknowledge beauty.
Be respectful to it and it will come again and again,
If only to confirm the reason why we are alive.

Change

Buttons fall
Revealing truth, pain and suffering.
The poor, the rich, the tycoons.

What fun to say that wealth hides the truth of poverty.
Here it is harder to say that poverty hides the truth of wealth.
It drips golden in branded names and ostentatious towers.

We are all in pain, we are all one.
The man who picks up your cigarette butt
To sell to his brother who works for you.

Cry little child
You are born to bring change.
The way is arduous and inherent.

No heart will comfort you.
Look not in our thoughts to take you home
But trust in the changelings of your soul.

A Time Will Come

A bright white time
Of metamorphosis
When the cross fades into our hearts.

When the beating of drums
Awakens our souls
Calling on all within to life.

Rivers of milk to nurture the poor,
Mountains of grain to feed the hungry,
Tenderness to quieten the fearful.

Hush my child
Peace is only a breath away
Where heaven is here on earth.

The time is nigh
When we will open our eyes
To the dawning of new beginnings.

We are all pilgrims to our destinies
When a smile leads our fate
And we surrender each step to Love.

A noble moment
Of God's love
Manifest in life.

Healing

With a fever hidden,
The pain grows;
Like silence that lies dormant
In unsuspecting corners within.

As the pages of life turn,
The book grows thicker.
The obscurity becomes pain itself,
And the healing drifts even further away.

So go to where the sediment lies thickest.
Taste the bitterness of one's hell.
Let the illness take form,
And utter the dreaded words of forgiveness.

Then wine will turn to water,
The fog shall clear,
The river will again begin to flow,
And expressions of transparency shall be spoken.

Holding Hands

Love the wanton child who travels alone;
Bless him for his fortitude.

Every day his prayer is one of return,
His only recourse; to stay alive.

His knowledge is clear
Yet of this world he comprehends little.

He seeks the honesty of man
To be his guide.

The more he moves about his life,
The stronger and more desperate becomes his nature.

Cherish him while he lives,
For a part of the wanton child lives in us all.

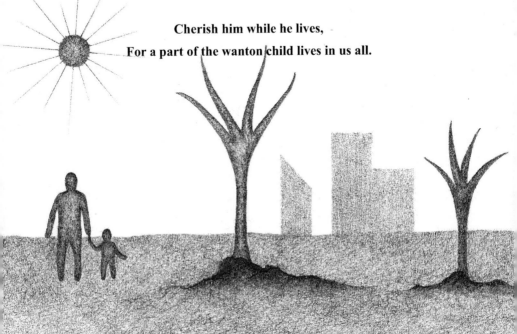

Faith In Courage

Feelings rot in festering unsaid truths.
They burn under the counsel of 'better left forgotten.'
Becoming putrid, icy memories that trickle painfully into the present.

Hard words take shape to express neglected love.
Love that heals the deepest recesses of any crevice,
Be it times past, present and future.

Love is the vibration of science's quantum physics.
A vibration unquantifiable, unseen,
But the source of all existence.

Our existence relies on our feelings vibrating with love.
Feelings touched by the spoken words of truth;
Unbiased, pure and simple.

Contd.

I wonder why it is so hard to live by that level of vibration.
Why is it so hard to feel without fear or awe?
Is it due to generations of those rotting unsaid truths?

Is that why it takes so much courage,
Courage to face the fear and anger in others,
Strength to accept the taste of their rot?

Is that why it takes ever more courage,
Courage to face my own fear and anger,
Even more strength to accept the taste of my own rot?

Tears can wash away a lot of pain.
Tears that come from the endless, forgiving well of love,
Come to help clean harsh judgements.

The endless well of love is in never-ending motion.
It exists.
We have all the help we want; we just need to feel it.

My Love

My sweetness, my love…
Can I find the words that plunge as deep as these emotions?
The depth where things are calm… still.
A stillness floating in open space.

A space so wide as to come full circle.
A symbiotic oneness with all things alive.
This is where the stillness is to be found.
This stillness that we have opened.

A stillness like taking a breath, taken for granted.
And yet, a place that can offer all the beauty we desire.
Where if we stop to listen we can hear life,
The finest, most pure vibration.

My sweetness, my love…
May this discovery never abandon me.
When the darkness envelops me may it be a thread of light,
A refuge that nothing existing can ever threaten.

Seasons

Twisting paths through the light of
Summer

Come together under the shade of
Autumn

To bury themselves in the earth of
Winter

Only to be reborn into the air of
Spring

Meandering Prayers

I wander aimlessly through the streets
Following the shadow of the setting sun.

My feet lead me to the park
Where I sit among the grass.

I dip my hands in a pile of autumn leaves
Feeling the exotic crunch of dry colour.

The cool wind runs across the ground
Lifting the leaves up around me.

I stand and gaze at the afternoon light,
The trees aflame in spires of celebration.

My lips quiver to the words of a prayer
In silent whisper to the coming of winter.

Newborn

A new birth,
The coming of life.

The greatest force of rapture,
The joy of life cradled in the arms of Love.

The strength of this elation,
The love of our soul.

Have it plant its roots in the earth,
Reaching for the Love of God.

Guardians to Love

We are guardians of this world,
Not only of the earth, but of ourselves.
It is not only for our descendants, but also our ancestors.

They stand among us watching and praying.
They look for our inner feeling;
To see how it has grown with wisdom.

They need our love, a pure and simple state of being.
They can taste it, like we taste sweet or bitter,
And like us, when they taste sweetness, it brings them joy.

This love can clear the confusion the mind likes to play with.
It can clear it because it holds no judgement.
It knows what is right and wrong because it is inside us.

And this is what we can give to our time.
This time when our mind likes to think it rules;
But it rules illusions when unaccompanied with a clear feeling.

The clearest feeling is love.
One that transcends time and space.
Believe in it; it has always believed in us.

The Jester

Safeguard the one who makes you laugh.
He may know of a sadness so dark, you would cease to exist.

The laughter he creates throws a shadow on sadness
Bringing light to those dark recesses in our minds.

Call him juvenile, silly or even unrealistic,
But if you can, look at the wisdom he brings.

He fights for justice.
The right for human beings to lift up their spirits.

Just think about how you feel when you laugh;
The space it frees up for inspiration.

It is his duty to fight that battle; he has no choice.
To open the doors of inspiration in others inspires him.

And are we not here to be inspired?
To feel what life is?

So when he asks you to laugh, laugh with him unashamedly.
The only thing he mocks is sadness.

Jewels

Melancholic dreams twitter in my ears.
A guide nudging me to see my sadness.
With a smile and a wink of reassurance, it tells me not to be afraid.

Taking me deeper, keeping a watchful eye on me,
I come to understand that sadness is not despair,
It is the deeper waters that hold up the happiness from which I drink.

It is not sadness, but a world in which lives the repercussions
of our lives.
In those waters swims all the things we do not want to see,
But look carefully and you can find jewels that shine without compare.

This is what all that melancholy is about,
Why it smiles while holding my hand.
It does not want me to feel hurt, but to find what shines brightest
in me.

Contd.

Sadness, like happiness, can be a cloud which hides ones truth,
But the jewels found have an inner light.
They contain the truths of who and why we are.

It is not an easy journey and requires more than one dive.
Like an inexperienced pearl diver, it is easy to drown.
Melancholy smiles as I begin to understand.

Wisdom comes with age that comes with many dives into those waters.
Fulfilment comes with courage, the courage to look for those jewels.
Liberty comes when we find enough jewels to free us of the passage
of time.

I squeeze melancholy's hand; I've had enough for now.
As we make our way back up, I look at myself.
I'm smiling as I take a mouthful of happiness.

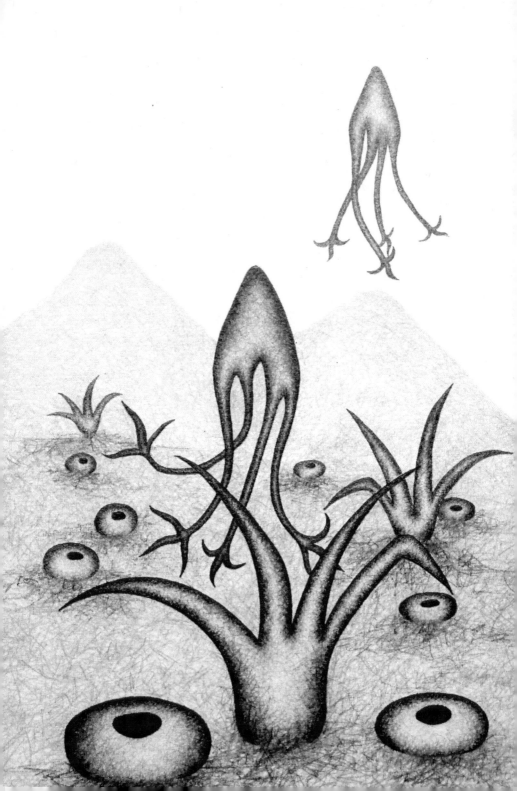

Lavender Dreams

Lavender dreams drift through time.
They weave the past and future into the present.
It tastes of love and feels like harmony.

Emotions forgotten in the sadness of our present.
Having no anchor, lavender dreams become lost,
Leaving us with the taste of hate and a feeling of anger.

How sad for us who believe in the tapestry of life,
A tapestry wide and rich in sensations.
Us who are stoned with words like unrealistic, dreamer, idealist...

We can not live very long with the ashen taste of despair,
When bitterness fuels our momentum.
We can only hurt humanity so much.

The tapestry of life is a living organism.
It will shift to mend the dropped stitch,
And when it does, lavender dreams will awaken mankind's rainbow.